The Lotus flower: A book of inspirational and healing poems

Terri Dorsey

BookLeaf Publishing

India | USA | UK

Presentation by *BookLeaf Publishing*

Web: www.bookleafpub.com

E-mail: info@bookleafpub.com

ISBN: 9789358316667

First edition 2024

DEDICATION

I want to dedicate this poetry book to my three children. I love you always!

PREFACE

The author of this book is a widowed mom of three and she is also a writer of poetry which she has used over the years as an outlet for emotions that she was unable to express verbally. When she is in need of this outlet, she picks up her pen and creates.

This has proven to be very therapeutic in her journey and she wanted to share it with you in hopes that it can help you heal also.

Straighten Your Crown

Though she is unsure of herself
She is confident in her ability
She's able to step into her divine energy Walking
with her crown confidently adjusted and
straightened
She is me, and I am her
The very epitome of a woman who is the vessel
of life
Using my powers for good, not evil

Return to Sender

My silence is loud
Loud enough that the whole world can hear
My thoughts penetrate my soul
Awakening every old wound
Every old cut and abrasion
I am not my past
So stop trying to make me live there
I have moved out leaving a vacancy with no
forwarding address
Stamping a return to sender because the new
address is unknown
Is my silence loud enough for you to hear
Do you understand the words unspoken
You did not keep me safe so I had no other
option but to start construction
The very construction that would build walls as
tall as the ceilings
Keeping all out who do not belong

Magnetic Energy for 2

As I greet you for the first time
Your energy pulled at mine
From the first words spoken so sweet
and soft
I could tell from the beginning your energy
spoke to me
It was definitely a feeling that I had never
encountered before
From the moment you walked through my door
From day one my heart and soul yearned
and ached for your sweet tender kiss
That was one thing now I truly miss
Remembering that I will never feel your touch
again
The energy that pulled me so close to you like a
positive to a negative has faded

Lost in Thought

The thoughts in my mind became overwhelming
like the running
of a treadmill to your destination
Expanding like the pressure of a sealed bag
when applying heat
Sometimes exceeding the capacity of the mind
The thoughts become blurs
You are constantly thinking but constantly
thinking about nothing
The muttering of the voices inside becomes an
echo of the deepest thoughts
Thoughts wanting to escape like a prisoner
behind bars
This voice is so loud you wonder if the whole
world can hear
The silent screams are abound

Just Friends

I tried time and time again to just be your friend

But you wanted more from me and it was plain
to see

We connected through a mutual friend

Not knowing love would become our end

Knowing it might be wrong

We could not stop the feelings within

Wondering if our love was enough for us to
survive

I did not want to be a secret in everyone's eyes

I want to be celebrated for the rest of our lives

WE CANNOT BE JUST FRIENDS

Deceit

When will I have a safe space
You claimed it was you
That lie just was not true
The words spoken tickled my ears
Yet the truth only proved false
False to the fantasy that it was you
You for me and me for you
Too bad it wasn't true

Addicted

The deep tingle that is felt from your head to
your toes
Pouring out like a fountain from the depths of
your soul
Even though love costs a high price
The soul still yearns for the highs
Anticipating the rush that I feel when I'm with
you
I don't want this feeling to end
Addicted and I can't kick this habit called you

Invisible

Yearning to be seen
Beyond the outer shell of the beauty that exists
Wondering will anyone ever dive deep enough
Seeing beyond the mesmerizing hazel eyes
Searching the darkness to reach the core
Understanding the reason for the pain
Comprehending the anger and hurt
Relieving her of this pain
And telling the little girl that lies within, take my
hand
Leading her out of the darkness to the light
Allowing her to run free, flaws and all
And still choosing to stay

In my Dreams

The memory of you has faded
Sometimes I can't remember your smell or even
your voice
When I close my eyes, you speak to me so clear
and it reminds me of yesterday
It is like time has stood still
Your smile so familiar now
Your touch still makes my heart skip a beat
Oh how I long to see you again
Until then I whisper,
See you in my dreams

Super Powers

I call it my super power
I have the ability to feel your energy when you
walk into a room
The fear of fitting in with all the strange faces
Wondering if you will be the odd one out
Not having a space to hide and cover up all your
insecurities
Can they see it on your face
I can see it in your eyes
Judgement of your choices or the places you
have been that you are unwilling to return
Sometimes with my super power I can breathe
the hurt that was not meant for me but intended
for you

Numb

The silence and pain penetrates
The feeling of emptiness burns a hole
Why is this life
Why is this my life
Loneliness is by my side
Walking with me every step of the way
Keeping close not allowing me to stray
Wrapping its arms around me so tight
Not allowing me to see the light

Secret to Happiness

What is Love
Is it the rush we get that makes it love
Love is only a word
A word that holds a lot of weight
Heavy like a bolder on your heart
I am terrified of this word
Even if it is just a word
It can be bittersweet
With all its highs and lows
I hope to one day overcome my fear of falling
Giving all of me not even worrying about
tomorrow
Is love just an illusion
Something that we fantasize about in our minds
Or is it the secret to happiness

Enough

You are enough
You were always enough
They just were wearing shades
Shades that blinded your greatness from their
eyes
The beauty and positive energy that you possess
The relationship was great because of you
You provided your feminine energy
The same energy they needed to meet Karma
My dear, you were always enough

Photo Album

From time to time I think of us
The memories that are etched into my soul
I think of you
I can still see your beautiful smile
Remembering your laughter allows me to think
of the good times
Those good times which were rare
I also remember when you raised your hand to
me
Making me feel less than what God intended for
me
Less than what my mom raised me to be
Allowing you to determine my greatness
I couldn't see the signs that were placed in front
of me
Just wanting to see the best in you
I could no longer see the good in me
My very essence was silenced by your evil
I am able to snap out of it and remember I
survived
While adjusting my crown I held my head high

You

It's you
You who was there to listen when I was
drowning
You who held me when I wanted someone
around
It's you who caressed me and touched me to fill
the void
The void that will always linger in the
background
We both carry that same void
Making space for this love to circulate
Allowing you to kiss me so soft and slow
Rubbing and caressing the things below
Giving much attention to places I can not
mention
At that point you are all mine
Probably because it's you and it's always been
you

Tunnel Vision

I am at a crossroads
My pathway is unclear
I shine my light to gain clarity
And to see what is near
I have searched for miles to see a glimmer of
light
While passing by the many distractions in the
darkness of the night
I stumble and trip over the many things sent to
destroy me
Conquering my fears of what lies before me
Gaining knowledge along my roadway to
withstand time
Hoping to one day see the light we all have
inside

My Mirror

The reflection I see in the mirror
I don't recognize
Her eyes have dark circles
Her hair is different colors now
The wrinkles need makeup to hide their frown
Why is she so unrecognizable
The clock has stolen her beauty
The beauty that she once could see
Is no longer where it used to be
I can see some similarities
But the reflection is still not me
Despite her reflection she is still that little girl
Longing for her mom to hold her and say
everything will be ok

Staying grounded

I can hear the sounds of the waterfall
Trickling down the jagged rocks
Seeing the reflection of the sunset on the water
Smelling the fresh honey suckles that have just
bloomed
Being mesmerized by the tiny ripples flowing
across the lake
Hearing the crickets sing a beautiful melody
This is my place to get away
The water becomes my peace
Allowing me to meditate on the day behind us
Manifesting the day ahead
Feeling the cool breeze touching my face
Letting the breeze blow away the worries from
today
I allow nature to ground me

Light Eyes

Some say her eyes are seductive
Others say her eyes are mysterious
Through her eyes she sees what you hide
She can see the deception way before the lie
Using her intuition to surpass the trials that are
set aside
Conquering every evil wishing on her demise
She is not just her pretty hazel eyes

Sorry

I'm sorry I can't be what you want
I'm sorry it's not the right time
Most of all I'm sorry you can't be mine
Lost in the energy and chemistry
Can you feel it like I do
That positive and negative push and pull
that happens between us two
I'm sorry there is not enough time
Most of all I'm sorry that I was blind
To the fact that you will never be mine
I'm sorry to myself because I knew the
consequences of our vibe

The growth of the Lotus Flower

The lotus flower grew from the roots at the
bottom of a pond
Although it grew from a place that was not so
great in the mud and murky water There was
beauty that came from the united mess
Sprouting to the surface the beauty that became
known as the aquatic perennial was like no other
Her unique beauty stood out from the rest of the
flowers
She only bloomed in the light of day and at night
was the darkest of dark
She had nothing but time at night to think about
what it took for her to show her beauty in the
light of the sun
she did not feel the beauty inside without her
colors and bloom
It was so dark at night that she felt invisible
Like there was forever between her and time
when someone would see her beauty
Finally the sun rises again to open up the petals
of her Lotus
She feels the sun and warmth upon her
This makes her feel whole again
She can be happy even if just for a short while

9 789358 316667